To: Cathy

Best wishes
Hope you enjoy

Bob
Woodruff

A
Wild Life
in
Worcestershire

The Nature of Poetry

Bob Woodroofe

Greenwood Press

*First published in 2024
by
The Greenwood Press
38 Birch Avenue
Evesham
Worcs. WR11 1YJ*

Tel 01386 446477

http://www.greenwoodpress.co.uk

Some of these poems have already been published in various poetry magazines & previous collections & performed at readings

Cover design & photographs Bob Woodroofe

Copyright © 2024 Bob Woodroofe

Bob Woodroofe has asserted his right under the Copyright, Design & Patents Act 1988 to be identified as the author of this work

*British Library Cataloguing-in-Publication Data
A catalogue record for this book
is available from the British Library*

ISBN 978-0-9957290-9-4

Introduction

All of the poems in this collection were
inspired by the wildlife of Worcestershire
in all its variety of shapes & forms.

Just random encounters with the ordinary flora &
fauna of our county's diversity that is there for all to find
if you take the time to stop and look.

Long may it remain and be treasured by us all.

Dedication

This collection is dedicated with grateful thanks to
all the hard work of the staff & volunteers of the

Worcestershire Wildlife Trust

without whom my home county of
Worcestershire would be so much the poorer.

Please note that all proceeds from the sale
of this book will be donated to the trust.

Reg. Charity Number 256618

Place

Where is this place, where I was born,
this midland shire, this market town.
This green garden upon the hill
to which I am rooted,
from which I have grown.

The soft contours of the Avon valley
flanked by Bredon's dome,
where the Vale blossom snows,
Cotswold beeches sigh on the ridge,
the Severn meadows silver with flood,
the cropped grass bleaches over Malvern rock.

It is here, I am home.

Contents

Flora 1
Birds 17
Fauna 33
Nature 49

Flora

Some of the plants that have given me such pleasure over the years in Worcestershire

A peal of flowers	*3*
After the storm	*4*
Alchemy	*5*
Leaf	*6*
Thorn	*7*
Open sesame	*8*
Belladonna	*9*
The Herb Garden	*10*
Pear	*11*
Pretence	*12*
Mace	*13*
Underneath	*14*

Spring - Cathedral Green - Worcester

A peal of flowers

A wash of bells peals through
the sunlit blue of anemones
ringing welcome to the light
shining bright on yellow celandines
from their leaves green glossiness
the first real breath of spring breathes
amongst the nodding daffodils
the air is filled with notes of bells
and see the bees visit for sweet nectar
flit from head to head dipping deep
the honey the bumble, the furry bee-fly
now yellow then blue and blue
blue amongst this sea of flowers
here and there a pure head of white
whilst all around the sounds spread
the flowers tremble slightly in the sun
is it the wind or the bells vibrations
that reach down into the ground
the bells that continuously sound
round and around round and around

The lake - Croome Park

After the storm

comes the intensity of stillness
the smell of damp earth rises
confetti petals litter the path
dripping trees flit with birds
swallows skim the meadows
weave through grass stems
the dandelion clocks are bare
time blown away
the scent of lilac and laburnum
bluebell and broom
and may
all mixed together
fresh green leaf boats drift
on the muddied waters
a collage of reed stems
blown into the lake corner
the still dark sky is lit
by a thousand candles
aflame on the horse chestnuts

Garden - Evesham

Alchemy

Air at dew point, water weighted,
pores secrete tears.
Held by a hair's breadth,
clear crystal perfect
reflective spheres
sparkled by a wind's waft,
mirror blue from flower's bed.

Blooms without petals, 8 winged stars,
cluster in tiny galaxies.
Haired velvet of toothed green
pleated with strong veins.
Cloaks that fold through the dark,
cover Transylvanian links,
spread silver from mountain moon.

From philosopher's stone,
prime element of creation,
poured from your leaves.
The summit of perfection,
celestial water, elixir of life,
transmute to perfect metal.
Our Lady's mantle.

Lady's mantle - Alchemilla mollis

All year round - Tiddesley

Leaf

Spring dawn cracks, the bud breaks,
nurtured within, the leaf wakes.
Unfurling into sharp morning air,
drawing virgin breath, unaware.
Mint green, proudly held aloft,
tender to air's touch, dew soft.
First blinding exposure to light,
burn of sun, hot and bright.

Watch and learn as the wind teases,
playing games, with childish breezes.
Through your veins rich sap flowing,
absorbing, producing, to adult growing.
Shade from noon's heat provided.
Growth to maturity safely guided.

Lifeblood, lifeline, severed, unwanted
chemical residues building, skin leathered.
Hanging, dying, freedom awaits,
dreams of flying, storm awakes.
The wind leaves the tree branches,
a single leaf, in its midst, dances
to earth, in evening calm, descended.
Finally fallen, a page, ended.

Layered memories piled high
under a growing dark sky.
Sunset frozen, eaten away,
dying, at the end of day.
Skeletal remains exposed
another year's chapter closed.

May - Cleeve Prior

Thorn

My time comes but once a year,
I follow the black and plum,
after my month I am named,
the only one.

I wear sweet trim of white
over my cloak of green,
freshness of petals budded tight,
promise of fruit to come.

My strange odour haunts the air,
smell the lust, taste the decay
that hangs from the hedges
in which I dance on my day.

Quick to grow I keep
the stock at bay, mark
boundaries, enclosures,
places where you meet.

Most celebrate of all,
sprung from Joseph's staff,
stand on the hill of Wearyall,
grace queen's table at Christmastide.

But you,
you must never
cast a clout till I am out
and never take me in.

Hawthorn - Crataegus monogyna

June - Eades Meadow

Open sesame*

Glimpse a view through blurred hedges each time you pass.
Slow, stop at the gate, lean on the five bars, ramshackle.
Look into sea of waving colour at history laid before you.
Grown and harvested for three hundred summers at least.
The hedge has marked the parish boundary for six centuries.
In seventeen seventy two your owner gave you his name.
Ghost of tillage shows in ancient roll of ridge and furrow.

There's no notice saying - Private - Keep out.
Why not climb over, wade waist deep amongst it all.
But something inside says - This is special - stop,
an unwritten law grown over time between you both.
After the hay is cut only the cows are privileged
to roam, crop sweet grass, rest in green oak shade,
share its bounty with the wild creatures that live there.

Once a year, the gate over which you stare so often swings open.
Welcome to a magic landscape of colour, shape and scent.
Tread gingerly between blooms, know that you trample life.
Delicate green veins, shades of deepest purple through to white,
Ragged pink, gold suns, frothing cream plumes.
Deeper in, from twinned leaves, rise green men on spikes.
Deeper still the single pale curve of leaf with reptile tongue.

After you have drunk deeply, cannot take any more,
close the gate softly behind you for another year.

* A means of acquiring or achieving what is normally unattainable (Oxford English Dictionary)

Summer - Cleeve Prior

Belladonna

You linger at light edge,
hide your dusky enchantment,
still subtly beautiful.

But what luscious black
devil's cherries you flaunt
to lure us to our fate.

We long to fill our mouths
with the tempt of you
yet know we dare not try.

Should you seduce the unwary,
should they succumb, bewitched
by your treacherous charms.

Then, with wide eyes,
accelerated hearts,
pulse weakening,

nerves numbed to oblivion,
they drift into your arms,
waiting, in the shadows.

Deadly Nightshade - Atropa belladonnana

Commandery Garden - Worcester

The Herb Garden

A thousand fingers point the way.
Steer the chariots drawn by doves
twixt devil's and dunny nettles.
Follow the trail the blue sailors sail.

Find jack behind the garden gate,
the herb of grace, the green ginger,
mary's milk-drops, the freckled face.
Beware marsh malice and snake's pie.

Listen to the church bells chime to
welcome the queen of the meadow.
Lad's love beds ladies in the hay,
fairy fingers pick their lockets.

Watch golden drops of evening fall
as long legs dampen in the dew.
The flicker of moth's moonflower
lit by the glow of evening star.

Cloister Garden - Worcester Cathedral

Pear

Spring promise of white blossom gone
grown to the hard green of small pears
browned and bletted they lie
ripe and scattered on the ground
almost turned to perry now
among the branches tangle and twine
dangle yellow leaves that soon will fall
long past the bright spring green
unfurled from sharp brown buds

the music of the bells vibrates
ring upon ring upon ring
blends to a continuous reel of sound
that peals around the cloister walls
sounds round and around and round
loosens the leaves tenuous hold
launches each on its own journey
long ships that sail gracefully away
on the wave of an autumn wind

the bright eyed robin sits and sings
his thin song drowned by bells
scented roses pink in pale sun
dew still fresh on the petals
silk strands tremble between the boughs
as the sun moves around the garden
edges slowly over the dial
we wait for spring to circle round
and blossom buds to break anew

Willow leaved weeping pear - Pyrus salicifolia pendula

September - Tiddesley wood

Pretence

Delicate paleness forces
through concrete ground.
Fragile shoot of softest cream
blooms at harvest, unadorned,
opens into mauve beauty,
lilac lined flecked with white.

Frenchmen call you "cul tout nu"
but you are too pure for that.
"Naked ladies" is more apt.
Fallow of bare earth between
the glossiness of green skirts
spring breezes lift each year.

Poison lily of damp fields
in season but falsely named,
a flavour of yellow colour,
dye from orange stigmas ground.
Insubstantial as petals
dashed to pieces by the rain.

Meadow saffron - Colchicum autumnale

The year round - Croome Park

Mace

there is a pool where the reed-mace grows
so quiet and lonely there
the bleached reeds sway to the breeze's touch
whisper their plaintive song
straw coloured stems in serried ranks
topped with chocolate cigars
sun flares across levelled mirror
to where the ditch drains away

here fluid waves over green star weeds
that reach up for the light
buoyant dabchick pops through surface film
ripples widen and spread
to green algal edge where moorhen nods
along her mazy trail
croak of spring bodies froth the liquid
to swelling mass of spawn

churr of warbler bounces bank to bank
cuts loudly through the air
come summer and robin's ragged pink
sparks bright among the reeds
alien spikes of purple orchids
make an almost foreign scene
dragons climb from dark deep into light
spread gauzy wings to fly

from steep burrowed bank the shy vole creeps
gnaws loud on juicy stem of reed
sentry heron forever patient waiting
still waiting stands
so the wheel turns water calms to glass
all is peace on the pool
the pool where the reed-mace grows turns quiet
so lonely there once more

Winter - all around the Vale

Underneath

The missile fashioned fired from a bow
aimed by an eye that couldn't see
slew his brother

A mother's tears rained down on me
from whence the arrow came
banished from the fletcher's realm
here suspended I must remain

Cut me as the year turns
take care for if I touch
the earth the magic drains
hang as the clock strikes twelve
before you burn the old

Be wary of the speckled bird
yet need him so you can fly
wipe sticky beak upon the bough
push my sinker in slowly bleed the tree

The legend lingers on
make the barren fertile
counteract the drug
pluck translucent berry
beware the kiss below

Mistletoe - Viscum album

Birds

The free spirits that fly the skies of Worcestershire

Rehearsal   19
Crescendo   20
Nog   21
We wait   22
The tiniest of birds   23
Slipstream   24
Terrorists   25
Spotted   26
A Robin   27
Summer's end   28
Singing leaves   29
Roost   30

Along the Avon - Evesham

Rehearsal

Streamside Alder burnt sienna catkinned.
Breast quivers light, piping Spring.

Repeat note, perfect performance, tune replay.
Reeds gleam, fluid tones ring over water gloom.

Flutes, phrases uttered, whistle showers.
Waves recited, flowing together.

Pouring forth soul to sky.
River echoes pure reprise.

Drop from branch. Voice winged away.
Recital over. Silence streams.

Song thrush - Turdus philomelos

Such a delight to hear them all - Croome Park

Crescendo

The clamour of daws greets you,
chuckle and swoop of fieldfares still here,
geese whoop and bark on the lake.

The click and whistle of coots,
white blaze arrowing the surface,
wings pattering the water.

The chaffinch sings his round,
greenfinches wheeze overhead,
the yaffle drums and laughs.

Swan heads move in unison,
dip, snake and rise, the cob mounts,
they stretch, point to sky, softly moan.

To the west buzzards hang and mew,
the first swallow cuts across air,
the motorway drones a world away.

Still haunting our waterways - River Avon - Evesham

Nog

Under the willow canopy
catkins of silk dress the river.
The ripple of water feeds
the sharp crave of hunger.
Stealthy movement creeps,
long shanks wade water.
lift.... slide.... place....
lift.... slide.... place....
The grey ghost pauses,
motionless,
above the sinuous eel.

The slow edge forward,
the lean closer,
eyes locked on.
Lean closer still.
The 'S' unwinds,
a lightning stab,
juggle and swallow,
slender neck bulges.
A slip of water washes down.
Then crouch, lift and away,
on arched wings, legs trailing.

Heron - Ardea cinerea

How we long for them each year - Evesham town

We wait

for crescent specks to scythe across sky
sickle winged silhouettes the anchor
that flies drops through blue ether

you who barely touch the earth a life aloft
borne on the wing the high drawn out squeals
of the cries of lost souls as you wheel overhead

last to come first to go the hotter the weather
the higher you rise until you descend
fly low when rain drives your food down

feed in a frenzy so we can hear and feel
the rush of curved wing that cleaves
through the air around our heads

drift up on thermals to your hammock
in the heavens upon pillow clouds dream
through darkness under summer stars

you couple on the wing plummet to earth
rocket up into our roof space scrabble
in darkness lay eggs raise young

barely fledged you stream away south
whilst we wait as days get shorter as air cools
around us we wait for your screams again

Swift - Apus apus

So wonderful to have seen this - Lower Moor

The tiniest of birds

came to my window
picking at insects
on the cotoneaster branch
a short distance from the glass

so intent on his reflection
he seemed oblivious of my presence
as I approached from the other side
only inches between us now

the constant flick flick of wings
his agitation obvious
the livid crest of gold raised
displaying his aggression

suddenly the light was cut
by the brown chequered bulk of a wren
looming behind him in the bush
and with a sudden start he was gone

Goldcrest - Regulus regulus

Such aerial acrobatics - Bredon Hill

Slipstream

Up where the wind waters eye,
a backdrop of hills, a sinking sun.
Four dark sails slide between clouds,
sweep and glide, scour the view,
drop deep into patchwork green.
A sudden rush, a glimpse, as
black rags flash past from below,
tossed by air streaming up scarp.
Watch as they slip, bank, stall,
tumble from sky, half closed,
split the draught with wings.
Circle on currents, swoop again,
rocket up once more.
Hear air buffet each feather
strain the barbs.
Sheer pleasure of wind
screaming through pinions
brings a deep throaty gurgle,
almost a chuckle, as they revel
in the exhilaration of pure play.

Raven - Corvus corax

They still manage to make it each year - Meadows - Lower Moor

Terrorists

grey ones hawk about the country
searching searching
she slips in plants the charge
unseen unseen

disguised to suit her special target
hidden hidden
a dozen time bombs to slavery
ticking ticking

the gentle shell kills by stealth
breaking breaking
a secret weapon in each home
growing growing

all opposition put to flight
routed routed
over the edge into oblivion
falling falling

he only sits keeps watch
calling calling
the twofold note from the hedges
echoes echoes

the infamous voice stops the bird has flown
silence silence
left to make their own way home
unknown unknown

Cuckoo - Cuculus canorus

Such a bright bird - Garden - Evesham

Spotted

Suddenly you materialise
grace us with your presence
not Spring, but fat August
a pause on your way south
from under yews deep shade
the intent watchful gaze
with dart twist flutter
you outmanoeuvre capture
the buzz of summer
turn on a feather
return to perch

by instinct or learning
your bright unblinking eye
found this oasis
in a concrete land
you cannot be the same
catcher of flies
a descendant perhaps
but you are here then
black eye searching
skies for African warmth
just as suddenly gone

Spotted Flycatcher - Muscicapa striata

To brighten all our days - Garden Evesham

A Robin

a robin sang in August
flung his song upon the air
it rose up from the garden
from his perch we knew not where

a blessing for us to hear
after a silent July
there really is no reason
why we should hold him so dear

with your red breast and bright eye
you lighten the wet and the cold
glad to share in your short life
we listen to your sweet song

sing loud from your perch on high
pour forth from the cherry bough
brighten each day with your song
sing on into Autumn's cool

tell all the world your story
cheer us during Winter's cold
till fresh Spring comes once more
lays her flowers at your door

let all know that you are here
know that you're always welcome
in our green garden's haven
so sing on sweet bird sing on

Robin - Erithacus rubecula

Always sad to see them go - Field Barn - Cleeve Prior

Summer's end

I've noticed you,
these last few days,
sat on the wire,
telling Summer's story
to your children.
Sun soaked days,
soaring high over the earth
on arced wings,
or skimming ground for food
in thunder showers,
exploding crystal rain drops
that ball and roll off oiled plumage.
Gathering strength for the journey,
storing it away to last,
to fuel the flight
that instinct senses.
One last twitter
as if goodbye,
slim body tenses,
you launch yourself,
gleaming blue steel,
circle once and away south,
trailing feather streamers.

Swallow - Hirundo rustica

Amazing to see and hear them - Trees - Croome Park

Singing leaves

they come
air darkens
clouds swirl and swoop
circle and alight
re-leaf treetops
with leaves that sing
that shuffle and shift
in non-existent breeze
sun sparkled breasts
glint in pale light
the whisper of a thousand tongues
beaks agape with gossip
spreads the news
clouds erupt as they leave
dissolve into silence
till only bare twigs remain
pointing to a cloudless sky

Starling - Sturnus vulgaris

Bedtime around the lake - Croome Park

Roost

high on the topmost twigs
fieldfares face into the wind
the tracery of branches blurs
as they flex in the blast
more chuck across the sky
fall headlong into trees
rapid wingbeats of a
mallard squadron circle
outlined by sinking sun
then drop to the dark lake
skid to rest on oily surface
a late heron stalks the shore
still fishes as gloom gathers
blackness of rooks trails home
ragged v's of gulls drift high above
the tighter v of canada's honks below
as dark and quiet descend to night

Fauna

The wonders of the animal world

Alien	*35*
Helix	*36*
Seeker	*37*
Bridge of shells	*38*
B is for	*39*
Lucky or not	*40*
Exuviae	*41*
Moth	*42*
New clothes	*43*
Cloister Garden	*44*
Riders of the film	*45*
Moth to the flame	*46*

So vibrant and alive - High Street - Evesham

Alien

How did it get here?
Invading the street, bristling on the path.

A lemon-yellow upturned brush,
flashing jet black from cracks that
open as it sinuates across the slabs.

The tufts threaten,
trail a warning red plume.

Such flamboyance, to turn,
into a drab creature of the night,
that cannot even eat.

Caterpillar of Pale Tussock Moth - Calliteara pudibunda

Spiral symmetry along the Avon - Pershore

Helix

Hogweed skeletons rattle
white in the wind with snails
banded brown and cream.

Each distinct from the other,
they clasp the hollow stems,
climb belly-footed to the light.

Creep up six, seven, eight feet,
exposed, no sustenance here.
a sitting target, clustered together.

The brittle stalks festooned
with their circular patterns,
with brown lips or white lips,

Cepaea nemoralis or hortensis.
such spiral adornment that
clings, that flings love darts.

In search of light - Garden - Pershore.

Seeker

Under the moon the bats flicker
between the tree branches,
swoop low over the pond,
where the hedgehog laps his fill.

Tiny concentric rings spread
over the reflected sky.

They say the butterfly
is the symbol of the soul,
what then is the moth,
that ghosts through the bushes.

Drawn to the window
this being whose lemon wings,
flutter against the pane,
seeking light.

Swallow-tailed moth - Ourapteryx sambucaria

Just how do they know? - The Bridges - Pershore

Bridge of shells

Down below the muddied waters swirl
and gurgle around the arch bases,
wear the ancient stone away.

Above the whirlpool of water
the brickwork is studded,
bristles all over with shells.

Snails, garden, brown lipped,
white lipped, unknown others,
all jostle for space.

Somehow, animal instinct
knows when danger threatens,
they just don't get caught.

But how long before did they
sense this flood so they could
inch upward to safety.

Keep pace with the rising water,
the whole bridge encased
in their living shells.

There are so many to enjoy - Garden - Evesham

B is for

Butterflies on Buddleia
the red and white of Admiral
orange and black of Tortoiseshell
jagged tawny of Comma
and Whites large and small

Bumble bees on Bergamot
Honey bees buzz on Borage
more Bumbles on Broad beans
and later on Runner beans

A huge droning hoverfly
lumbers in to feed
brown and yellow banded
mimicking a hornet

Birds on the Silver Birch
Blue tits search every branch
the ubiquitous Blackbird
rose breasted Bullfinch

Every morning and evening
the blur of whirring wings
as Humming bird hawk moth
hovers at the tiny purple trumpets

Butterfly transect - Windmill Hill

Lucky or not

Fed well on trefoil and vetch
the poison molecules stored
winter lost amongst the grass
then climb their thin ropes
spin silk to parchment
swell the narrowness of stems
the shucked black skin
crumbles between fingers
ash spread on the wind
in the light of day not night
whirring warning into flight
crowd and jostle to feed
on blue scabious purple knapweed
magenta spots on deepest black
red for danger six for luck

Six-spot Burnet moth - Zygaena filipendulae

The magic of metamorphosis - Garden pond - Evesham

Exuviae

you lurked in the murky depths
a hook jawed savage monster
that ravaged your watery world

now you emerge into air
climb a stem and wait
till your back splits asunder

struggle out of constricting skin
the spoils of the enemy
stripped from your own body

all that's left the sloughed skin
empty and abandoned
a dry husk brittle to touch

now a magnificent creature
with eyes that flash
wings that glitter rattle in the wind

a darter or darning needle
to stitch the eyelids of sleepers
should they rest by the stream

an adder bolt or horse stinger
a skimmer a chaser a hawker
devil's riding horse or snake doctor
or even an emperor

Emperor Dragonfly - Anax imperator

Running on fumes - Garden - Pershore

Moth

Beat the night,
silently,
on scaled wings,
trawl air seas for scent.

Relentlessly
search, rest at dawn,
and as dark drops
launch yourself once more.

Probe for the molecule,
the gaseous atom
that registers on feathered antennae,
that your heightened senses track.

Trail the waft that tantalises,
home in till you trace
the source, and the vapour
explodes in your brain.

His Majesty - Tiddesley Wood - Pershore

New clothes

open wide the iris of your eye
when you go to the woods today
through the aperture have vision to view
he who fed from the spreading sallow

yet now he rises to the tallest oaks
hunts a mate through leafy green
see him fight flash bright in sun
then quench his fire from puddles

drawn down to the rottenness of life
now dressed in resplendent brilliance
the purple sheen unparalleled
lights his grand imperial majesty

Purple Emperor - Apatura iris

How do they do it? - Cloister Garden - Worcester Cathedral

Cloister Garden

Bees congregate over lavender, bees that shouldn't be able to fly, that are aerodynamically unstable, but fly they do, and even hover. Bumble bees with buff tails. Bombus for their humming sound, terrestris for of this earth, they buzz amidst their purple heaven.

Molecules of aromatic gases released from flowers draw them in, up and over the cathedral's walls. Ultraviolet lines on petals act as landing lights, point the way that leads to the sweetest of prizes. They touch down, leave scent on petals, long tongues sip nectar.

When flowers carry a hint of a previous bee's lingering presence, sensed through the soles of their feet, then they pass these by. They fly through air positively charged, land on negative flowers, the pollen attracted to them carried from one bloom to another.

Thus each flower is fertilised, fair trade for nectar carried home to feed the next generation. Their only dilemma which to visit next.

Buff tailed Bumble Bee - Bombus terrestris

Fascinating creatures - Garden pond - Evesham

Riders of the film

Molecular force holds the meniscus,
pulls it into the liquid body, as you
skate over the tensioned skin.

Pads of hair dent the surface,
repel and push the fluid down,
never sink in, never get wet.

Four indentations cast shadows
that float over the sunlit bottom
as you scull over the film.

Sense the vibrations, ripples
that spread from prey that drowns,
stride over to suck it dry.

Fly to winter shelter,
in spring return,

walk once more on water.

Common Pond skater - Gerris lacustris

What wonderful names - All around Worcestershire

Moth to the flame

I was confused, uncertain, but always suspected
the old lady, mother shipton, with her hooked snout.
A non-conformist, bit of a gypsy, some say a sorcerer.
Her death's head rearing upward like the phoenix.

She who lives on the marsh, down by the rivulet,
under the dark arches of chestnut and sycamore.
With the bleating goat, the kitten under the alder,
ear always cocked, listens for the beat of a mouse's heart.

Her grey feline ghost constantly sweeps with her broom,
mumbles in a tongue like Latin, under a crescent moon.
The fox's brown tail in the fern, leads the forester
round and around in figures of eight or eighty.

She lays out the red carpet for the traveller.
Kindles the brimstone to spark alight the wood.
The flames herald first the autumnal fires,
close followed by December and winter's cold.

The rustic stranger with his scallop shell,
he who greets her with a bright wave,
uses language to more than make a maiden blush,
always has the luck of the chimney sweeper.

A drinker of dew, an emperor, living in exile,
with a black neck, but the grace of a leopard.
The belted beauty whose burnished brass buckle glints,
adorned with both the bird's wing and deer antler.

The green silver lines of the gem in the V of her throat
catches the oblique stripe of light from spluttering candle.
A cream wave of wax shapes a yellow shell with yellow tails,
the bead of her brown line bright eye fixed on the spectacle.

Nature

Worcestershire in all its wild glory

First	*51*
Dead Man's Ait	*52*
Blossom time	*53*
April showers	*54*
Headstones	*55*
The Vale	*56*
The Wood of Tidi	*57*
B-brooks	*58*
September sun	*59*
Eel	*60*
Castle	*61*
Hipton	*62*

I hope they still keep coming and going - Worcestershire

First

we wait each year
for those that stay
the first snowdrop
catkins on the hazel
the first butter coloured fly
cherry plum blossom

we wait each year
for those that go
the honk and V of skeins of geese
the grey backed farewell chuckle
the last flash of scarlet underwing
the wing creak and yellow beak of whoopers

we wait each year
for those that come
the first chiff-chaff the first cuckoo
that flash and twitter of blue cutting blue
that scream of joy arcing across the sky
and hope for painted ladies and clouds of yellow

The wildlife still remains - River Avon - Evesham

Dead Man's Ait

You always look so peaceful and calm,
your reed fringed waters full of charm.
The river in its banks gently sleeved,
evening mist over your water wreathed.

The badger over the meadow wends his way,
treads well-worn paths through stems of hay.
The owl floats ghostly over the mist,
white feathers by late beams of sunlight kissed.

The fox, disturbed by hunger from his lair,
pads slowly down the path, sniffs damp air.
He stops to slake his thirst from your bank,
sends voles rustling through rushes rank.

Pushes his nose through fringing grass,
sees the moon reflected as if in glass.
The ripples from his tongue gently spread,
rocking the moon and stars to bed.

Your waters, home to pike and eel,
quietness broken by angler's winding reel.
Moonlight glitters off gossamer line,
a thread descends deep to ancient time.

Long ago your stream ran red,
fierce battle raged, much blood was shed.
Ghosts still linger in your tranquil backwater,
mute witness to that ancient slaughter.

But still all the creatures come and go
to use your waters that still run slow.
To drink, to feed, you serve them all,
quietly wait to hear the otter's call.

Still amazing to see every year - Evesham Vale

Blossom time

The Vale in Spring, blossom time,
like a bride, so pure, so fine.
It wears its veil, decked out in white,
draped over the hills, what a sight.
Virgin white, tinted with fresh green
as leaves unfurl, complete the scene.
Wind blown snowstorms at a glance,
petals falling softly, down they dance
onto the bright green sward to lie,
like God's confetti from on high.
Gazing down from Hipton high,
Vale lit by sun from azure sky.
Black barn like upturned boat,
lost in sea of foam, afloat.
Fragile blooms holding future life,
frost cuts at them like a knife.
Full of promise of things to come,
sweet fruits of apple, pear and plum.
Each year we wait to see this sight,
nature so simple, yet pure delight.
Each year our hearts for blossom yearn,
may such a sight for ever return.

An incredible snowfall - Evesham

April showers

the thrush serenades us in morning rain
as he has done since late February
we look for him on favourite perches
maybe sheltered somewhere
trying to keep his feathers dry

and then the rain slowed down
I don't mean that it eased off
but its descent slowed down
before our eyes it changed
slowed to sleet then further

it whitened slowly to snow
flakes coalesced in clumps
almost weightless they drifted
floated softly down
coasted to the ground

the sight even silenced the thrush
all you could hear was the
soft rustle of the flakes
as they jostled each other
in their slow descent

we went outside to try to catch
these fragile featherweights
but somehow they evaded
our outstretched hands
to melt away on the ground

Life and death together - Hampton Church - Evesham

Headstones

the drive a winding path bramble overhung
through rusted gates cow parsley showers
speckled wood shies in dappled light
then spirals madly into sky
starlings bustle through grass tufts
between graves lain under flowering thorn
hooded jackdaw watches from the tower

under the church clock bluebells strike the hours
nourish a small tortoiseshell's sweet appetite
blown beech bud sheathes pile the path
a cuckoo calls both notes clear and true
orange tips seek 'jack by the hedge'
yew's flaked red flavoured bark
shelters in its own deep shade

flowers butterflies birds trees
all these I name
spirits of life among the dead
like the names carved on stone
they mean nothing unless known and
each has grown its own association
particular to me

From the top of Windmill Hill nature reserve

The Vale

tufts of old mans beard wave
silver in sunlight against blue sky
tall spears of mullein sway
shower seed along the verge
secret beneath the soil lie
the balled roots of orchids
sunlight stored ready
to send up spotted leaves
and pink pyramids next year
a kestrel glides on thermals
banks and slips along the ridge
hangs on quivering wingtips
then drops like a stone
buzzards ride the updraught
flight paths criss and cross
as they circle up and up
the swollen river tumbles over
the weir into a froth of
swirling brown foam
rushes away downstream
across the plain the humped
whale of Bredon rises
crowned by tree and tower
gazes down across the Vale

The wonders of ancient woodland - Pershore.

The Wood of Tidi

Sink into quietness as you enter,
wooded since the age of ice,
Tidi worked here 800 years ago.
Huge old coppice stools, moss coated,
multi trunked, proclaim it so.

First bells of blue scent the spring,
the twin leaves of the twayblade,
the four leaves of the paris herb.
Followed by the devil's bit blue
and meadow saffron's lilac hue.

See the peacock on the nettles
vie with tortoiseshell and comma,
and orange tips on jack by the hedge.
The tawny fritillary dashes down the ride
as speckled woods dance in dappled shade.

The ride now a riot of yellow, purple, cream.
evening primrose, fleabane, meadowsweet,
scented agrimony, marsh thistle, willowherb.
Small teasel, loosestrife, blackberry blossom,
where white admirables glide down to feed.

The noble chafer still roams the orchards,
on the ranges the badger excavates his sett,
wanders off along his ancient trackways.
The crack of rifles is no longer heard
and bees mine the sand, not bullets.

In the wood a 'fall' of trees new felled,
brash protects from gnawing teeth of deer.
Tall oak 'whitepoles' left to cut 14 years from now,
taller oak 'blackpoles' left to cut a further 14 years on,
and so the cycle continues round.

And still they flow - Evesham

B-brooks

We're certainly not much to look at as we wander along our way,
not the beautiful babbling kind, your quintessential tinkling stream.

We've a grubby kind of look, flow under roads and around houses,
don't flow serenely by, sometimes we trickle, sometimes we gush.

We're not deep, but rather shallow, run over bricks and rubble,
flow between our banks through the thrown in shopping trolley.

Each and every time it rains we turn this slightly milky hue,
used to the pollution, we just let it go, flush it straight through.

Look In Spring and you'll see celandine stars line our banks glow
yellow in warming sun, and see how our sparkling waters run.

Brambles across the stream give blackberries at Summer's end.
bright hips and haws, lit by Autumn light, hang over our banks.

Ivy flowers for butterfly and bee, our berries for all the winter birds,
fallen trunks span the stream, invite the adventurous to cross.

You can still find odd places where loach and minnow swim,
see that flash of blue, a darting kingfisher just whistled through.

We're all B's, Broadway, Badsey, Bengeworth and Battleton too,
trace our source, follow the course of each of us separately.

It's plain that we're all contributory and we all eventually join up,
go down to the Avon, then the Severn, off to the sea and away.

Be thankful for the sun - Croome Park

September sun

Footprints mark your passage
through the dew on the grass.
In the soft breeze tendrils of mist
wreathe and linger over the lake.
Jewelled cobwebs spread over every branch,
glisten and tremble in the air.

On the bank the chocolate velvet
of reed mace smooth to the touch
spear up through the green blades.
A heron ghosts silently from the shore,
The swirl and splash of a feeding pike
breaks the lake's mirrored calm.

See the shiny brown sheen of chestnuts,
freshly sprung from cream velvet
lining of spiny green cases.
Squirrels tail chase around the trunks
Unseen jackdaws clamour from
their roost in the top of the plane.

Across the park the guttural croak
of raven answers through the mist.
Nuthatches flute loudly from the trees,
a wren fires from the undergrowth.
A darter lands on the white wing
of a feeding swan and suns itself.

The warmth brings out the butterfly,
the dragonfly from its reed shelter,
wings aglitter in the sunlight.
In the meadow sheep contentedly graze
the lush re-growth, jackdaws
riding on their backs. The sun
has brought the world to life again.

Long may they still return - River Avon - Evesham

Eel

fish with no scales mucus slippery
writhe silver in storm moons light
glide through wet grass breathe through skin
exist on stores of fat unable to feed
from pond and stream answer the craving
drawn down by the tidal urge
hungry for salt and sex
plunge to the sea and west
over the shelf to depths of darkness
lengthened by the shift of continents
a journey to die for no return

life prevails from wasted bodies
spawned deep in the sea of weeds
they rise up drift on currents
feed and grow reach the coast
slivers of glass through channel tides
shoaling Severn Sharpness Frampton
Newnham beyond slip nets climb weirs
Wainloads Tirley Apperley on
to where ancestors lived and dreamed
Tewkesbury Bredon Evesham home
each imprinted in their genes

Bredon Hill - from Elmley Castle.

Castle

Sunlight filters through golden leaves
that still cling fast to the spreading oaks
by the stream that flows underneath
the wagtail chip-chips as she flits away

the old stile leads off into the field
striped green rows of winter wheat
march up the slope towards the hill
where bright pheasants strut and preen

the castle above is divided by slants of light
luminous green ramparts edged in dark ditches
from the treetops jackdaws chack as they
launch themselves to sport in the updraught

spider skylines waft lazily in the breeze
while the silk netted grass glistens below
a lone figure trudges slowly around the field
follows the pathway that winds on and up

past the castle and through the dark woods
labours on to the very top and the tower
to be rewarded on a day such as today
when the seven counties must surely be in view

The magic of murmuration - the Lenches

Hipton

Out in the quietness of evening fields
long tufts of grass pull at our legs
as we wade through them
towards the overgrown hedge.
Towards the brambles that snake
around our shins, trip us up,
scratch our outstretched arms.

We filled punnet after punnet,
that bubbled over with the black fruit.
Purple fingered we watched
spellbound as the huge orange ball
dropped towards the hill.

Dark clouds suddenly settled over us,
moved first one way, then the other.
Blotted out the setting sun, the whirr
of thousands of wings ever louder.

Trees grew more and more leaves,
whistles and calls grew in volume,
till dumbstruck we staggered
back across the fields and out
of the deafening murmuration.

Watched and listened till all
was quiet and still and as
the sun finally sank beyond the hill,
we carried our black bounty home.

Starling - Sturnus vulgaris

Who would have thought that

Wood Whites would flutter again
along Monkwood rides
Brown Hairstreak thrive in Grafton
Silver Washed Fritillaries and
Purple Emperors grace Tiddesley

Buzzards would ride our thermals
once more mewing from the blue
the 'cronk' of Ravens sound overhead
Red Kites soar over Bredon and our towns
the white purity of Egrets grace our wetlands

Scarce Blue Tailed, Willow Emerald
and Keeled Skimmers would reach us here

The Balsam the Bees love
would smother our wetland flowers
the Box Tree Moth that is so attractive
would decimate our bushes

We'd have Grasshoppers on our front lawn
and even Bee Orchids in the back

Who knows what the future holds

Could Beavers dam our waterways
Lynx hunt in the woods
Wolves roam over our hills

About the Author

Born & bred & still living in the Vale of Evesham Bob Woodroofe's poems appear in many poetry magazines & are performed locally. Inspired by the natural world, the landscape & local tradition he attempts to bring the magic of nature & its restorative & healing qualities to a wider audience.

Also available from the

Greenwood Press

38 Birch Avenue, Evesham
Worcs. WR11 1YJ

website http://greenwoodpress.co.uk

e-mail info@greenwoodpress.co.uk

by Bob Woodroofe

*A trilogy of poetry collections from
life & nature in the Vale of Evesham*

Nature, Reflections & Spirit of the Vale

In search of greenness

Something Stirred

A trilogy of Poetry Collections

Pick of the crop, Another Lad of Evesham Vale & Plumlines

*Joint poetry collections by
Sue Johnson & Bob Woodroofe*

Tales of Trees, Journey & Pathways

*Creative Writing books
by Sue Johnson*

Writer's Toolkit & Writer's Toolkit 2, 3 & 4

Printed in Great Britain
by Amazon